D0343464

How Smart Are You?
TEST YOUR MATH IQ

How Smart Are You?

TEST YOUR
MATH IQ

Discover Your Math Aptitude
and Sharpen Your Skills

THOMAS J. CRAUGHWELL

BLACK DOG
& LEVENTHAL
PUBLISHERS
NEW YORK

Published by
Black Dog & Leventhal Publishers, Inc.
151 West 19th Street New York, NY 10011

Distributed by
Workman Publishing Company
225 Varick Street New York, NY 10014

Manufactured in China
Cover and interior design by Elizabeth Driesbach

ISBN-13: 978-1-57912-903-3
h g f e d c b a
Library of Congress Cataloging-in-Publication Data available upon request

CONTENTS

For Sean F. Nolan
Hell has frozen over.

INTRODUCTION

Everyone remembers the math wizards from school—the kids that unsnarled the most tangled word problems, never confused area with radius, and were always the first ones to discover the value of x. For many of us, however, decimals, fractions and algebraic equations tended to overheat our tender young brains. And that's a shame—because there is genuine pleasure is working through and finding the solution to a math problem. It builds up one's concentration, sharpens the mind, and reinforces problem-solving skills.

This book contains 50 quizzes with a total of 500 math puzzles that range from calculating the angles of a triangle to working out compound interest. We've selected puzzles for a variety of skill levels, so some of the questions are more challenging than others. At the beginning of each section, you'll find brief bios of groundbreaking mathematicians to inspire you. In the back of the book and at the end of some chapters, you'll find a few blank pages where you can work out equations.

Wherever you fall in the spectrum of math wizards, you'll find quizzes that stretch your math muscles, entertain you, and brush up skills you haven't used since middle school. So sharpen your #2 pencils and dive in!

CHAPTER 1

WORD PROBLEMS

Pythagoras
(c. 578-505 BC)

In the ancient world, the Babylonians were renowned for their discoveries in astronomy and the Egyptians for their understanding of the principles of engineering (how do you think they built the pyramids?). So Pythagoras, a young man with an avid interest in understanding how the universe worked, studied with the best teachers he could find in Babylon and Egypt.

Although we are listing Pythagoras here among the greatest mathematicians, his interests went beyond numbers. He concluded that the world was a globe. He believed that thought was an activity of the brain, not (as was believed at the time) of the heart. It's said that he invented the words "philosophy" (from the Greek for "love of wisdom"), and "mathematics" (from the Greek for "subject of instruction," which is a far less catchy term than "love of wisdom").

In spite of his many interests, Pythagoras became primarily a numbers guy. He discovered and proved what has since been known as the Pythagorean Theorem, an equation we all learned in high school about a right-angled triangle: $a^\wedge + b^\wedge = c^\wedge$. Pythagoras' Theorem is believed to be the first geometric proof.

Pythagoras became enchanted not just by the elegant logic of numbers, but also by their beauty. It is said that he developed a kind of mystical religion that involved numbers, music (because the eight notes of the musical scale—do, re, mi, fa, sol, la, ti, do—can be expressed mathematically), the nature of the cosmos, and reincarnation—a belief that after death the soul of the deceased returns to earth to live in a new human body.

Pythagoras' mystical notions are little more than curiosities these days, but his mathematical discoveries are fundamental to our understanding of numbers and geometry.

✏️ Word Problems 1

1 Three bags of apples and two bags of oranges weigh 32 pounds. Four bags of apples and three bags of oranges weigh 44 pounds. All bags of apples weigh the same. All bags of oranges weigh the same. What is the weight of two bags of apples and one bag of oranges?

2 Over the course of four consecutive nights, a bat ate 1050 mosquitoes. Each night the bat ate 25 more mosquitoes than on the previous night. How many mosquitoes did it eat each night?

3 Ellie took her pulse and found that her heart beats at a rate of 80 beats per minute. How many days will it take for Ellie's heart to beat one million times. Hint: the answer will be x number of days plus a few hours.

4 The Yellow Cab Company charges $1.50 for the first mile, and 90 cents for each mile thereafter. A passenger has $20. He plans to give the driver a $2 tip. How many miles can he travel with the remaining $18?

5 A farmer sells 196 pounds of potatoes to a grocer. The grocer divides the potatoes into 5-pound bags and 2-pound bags. When he was finished, the grocer found that he had the same number of 5-pound bags as 2-pound bags. How many bags of each size did he use?

6 Jerry sells coffee mugs in two sizes, large and small. He sells the large mugs for $5.75 each, and the small mugs for $2.50 each. When he opened his mug shop he had a total of 200 mugs. When he closed the shop he had sold 12 mugs and made $56. How many mugs of each size did he sell that day?

7 Four families brought the same number of chairs to a neighbor's cookout. When all 27 invited guests arrived, the hosts discovered they were three chairs short. How many chairs did each family bring?

8 Aaron covers 15 miles a day on his raft. He sleeps aboard the raft, and every night the river's current pushes him 3 miles back. Aaron wants to reach a town 84 miles away. How many days will it take him?

9 Sarah's parents pay her to do odd jobs around the house. If she does a good job, she receives $3.33 for that day. If she has done an outstanding job, she receives $6.33. During one 10-day period, Sarah made $42.30. How many days did she do outstanding work?

10 A cook buys potatoes in 5-pound bags. Each 5-pound bag holds 20 potatoes. The cook uses 2 potatoes for each order of French fries. He charges 95 cents for each order of fries. How much money did the cook make on a day when he used 400 pounds of potatoes?

ANSWERS ·

① A bag of apples weighs 8 pounds. A bag of oranges weighs 4 pounds. 2 bags of apples and 1 bag of oranges weigh 20 pounds.

② 225, 250, 275, 300

③ 9 days

④ 19 miles

⑤ 28 5-pound bags and 28 2-pound bags

⑥ 4 small mugs and 8 large mugs

⑦ 6 chairs

⑧ 7 days

⑨ 3 days

⑩ $760

SCORING $\cdots\cdots\cdots\cdots\cdots\cdots\cdots\cdots\cdots\cdots\cdots\cdots\cdots\cdots\cdots$

Award 16.5 points for each correct answer.

165 Genius
148–132 Gifted/Superior Intelligence
115 Higher Than Usual Intelligence
99 Average Intelligence
83 Low Average Intelligence
70 or below Very Low Intelligence

✏ Word Problems 2

❶ Five quarts of blood passes through your heart every 60 seconds. A swimming pool holds 63,000 gallons of water. How many weeks will it take for your heart to pump 63,000 gallons?

❷ A family is shopping for a television. Three local retailers are advertising sales on televisions. The department store offers 20% off the retail price of $200. The electronics store offers 30% off the retail price of $180. The big box store offers 10% off, plus an additional 20% off the retail price of $210. Which store offers the lowest price and what is it?

③ In 5 days Nathanial ate 100 cookies. Each day he ate 6 more cookies than he had eaten the day before. How many cookies did Nathanial eat on the first day?

④ Elizabeth has $500 in her bank account. Sally has $200 in her bank account. Every week Elizabeth withdraws $15 but Sally deposits $12. At the end of 13 weeks, what is the balance of their two bank accounts?

⑤ High school biology students drew water from a local pond and found that their sample contained 45 minnows for every 27 tadpoles. In a second, larger sample they found 315 minnows. How many tadpoles were in the second sample?

⑥ A fudge shop goes through 15 pounds of chocolate, 30 pounds of sugar, and 21 pounds of butter every 3 days. In 3 weeks the shop is completely out of chocolate, sugar, and butter. How many pounds of each ingredient will the shop owner order to replenish his stock?

⑦ Tyler does not recycle. Every year he throws in the garbage 60 pounds of recyclable material. In how many years will Tyler have thrown away 1 ton of recyclable material? Estimate to the nearest whole number.

⑧ A gardener has found a hybrid that grows freakishly large eggplant. On the first day the gardener measured his eggplant, it was 6 inches long. The second day it was 15 inches long. Every day the eggplant grew by the same amount, plus inches. On what day will the eggplant be more than 11 feet long?

⑨ A woodworker specializes in 3-legged stools and 4-legged tables. In one month he used 72 legs and in the end had 3 more stools than tables. How many stools and tables did he build?

⑩ Loggers in the Amazon rainforest can cut down 100 trees per minute. How many trees will they cut down in a week?

ANSWERS ·

① 5 weeks

② The electronics store, $126

③ 8 cookies

④ Elizabeth's balance is down to $305; Sally's balance is up to $356.

⑤ 189 tadpoles

⑥ 105 pounds of chocolate; 210 pounds of sugar; 147 pounds of butter

⑦ 33 years

⑧ Day 9

⑨ 9 tables and 12 stools

⑩ 1,008,000 trees

SCORING ·

Award 16.5 points for each correct answer.

165 Genius
148–132 Gifted/Superior Intelligence
115 Higher Than Usual Intelligence
99 Average Intelligence
83 Low Average Intelligence
70 or below Very Low Intelligence

✏️ Word Problems 3

1. Dave and Gary have a lawn mowing business. Dave owns a riding mower and charges $18 per lawn. Gary has a walking mower and charges $20 per lawn. Dave can cut 9 lawns a day. Gary can cut 8 lawns a day. How much is each partner making per day?

2. On Thanksgiving, Mrs. Batali pre-heated her oven for 10 minutes and roasted her turkey for 4 hours and 15 minutes. The turkey has been out of the oven, resting, for 20 minutes. It is now 5pm. At what time did Mrs. Batali put the turkey in the oven?

3. Lizzie is baking a cake. The recipe calls for 4 cups of sugar. The only measuring cups she can find are the 1/2 cup and the 3/4 cup. Using both measuring cups, what is the least number of scoops she can make to reach 4 cups?

4. A cabin wall is 9 feet high. Every day a snail climbs 30 inches up the wall, but at night the snail slides back 12 inches. How many days will it take the snail to reach the top of the wall?

5. Mariah enjoys long walks. She walks 2 miles per hour uphill, 6 miles per hour downhill, and 3 miles per hour on flat ground. If she walked for 6 hours, how many miles did Mariah walk?

6. A classroom has an equal number of girls and boys. When 8 girls left to play soccer, there were twice as boys as girls in the classroom. How many students are in the class when everyone is present?

⑦ A store sells candy by the piece. One type costs 35 cents a piece; another costs 30 cents a piece. Joe spent $22.75 on an equal number of each type of candy. How many pieces of candy did he buy?

⑧ Lauren picked four numbers out of a hat. After adding up the four numbers, she found that the average was 9. Three of the numbers are 5, 9, and 12. What is the fourth number?

⑨ Jeff rented a car for a 2200 kilometer road trip across Canada. The car holds 24 gallons of gas. The car gets 27 kilometers to the gallon. Jeff began the trip with a full tank of gas. How many stops must he make to complete his road trip?

⑩ In a town election, the Republican candidate received 542 votes, the Democrat received 430 votes, and the Independent received 130 votes. Ninety percent of eligible voters turned out for the election. What is the total number of eligible voters in the town?

ANSWERS ·

① Dave makes $162 per day. Gary makes $160 per day.
② 12:15 pm
③ 4 3/4 cups; 2 1/2 cups
④ 6 days
⑤ 22 miles
⑥ 32 students
⑦ 70 pieces of candy
⑧ 10
⑨ 3 stops
⑩ 1224 voters

SCORING ·

Award 16.5 points for each correct answer.

165 Genius
148–132 Gifted/Superior Intelligence
115 Higher Than Usual Intelligence
99 Average Intelligence
83 Low Average Intelligence
70 or below Very Low Intelligence

✐ Word Problems 4

1. Maddy has 24 pencils, which she sells for 15 cents each. At the end of the day she has 8 pencils left. How many pencils did she sell and how much money did Maddy make?

2. The O'Brien family is going to buy a used car for $5800. The dealer offers them two options: they can pay the entire purchase price of $5800 in cash, or they can pay $1000 now and $230 a month for 24 months. How much more than the original price of $5800 will the O'Briens pay on the installment plan?

3. A sheet of paper is .01 mm thick. The sheet is cut in half and one piece is placed on top of the other. These two sheets are cut in half and the four pieces are piled up. After the 10th cut and pile process, how high will the pile be in mm?

4. A dry cleaner has raised her price for dry cleaning a jacket from $4 to $5. She will raise the price for dry cleaning a coat by the same percentage. If the old price for cleaning a coat was $10, what is the new price?

⑤ Alex has twice as many comic books as Steve. Steve has two-thirds as many comic books as Mike. Mike has 27 comic books. How many comic books does Alex have?

⑥ A department store bought men's handkerchiefs 6 for $10 and sold them 4 for $10. The store made a $60 profit. How many handkerchiefs did the store sell?

⑦ Grace is reading a 445-page book. She has read 157 pages. If she reads 24 pages a day, how many days will it take Grace to finish the book?

⑧ A cheese store sells cheddar cheese for $1.70 a half pound. How much does the store charge a customer who asks for 2.5 pounds of cheddar?

⑨ The record for sit-ups is 17,000 in 7 hours and 27 minutes. If a challenger did 40 sit-ups per minute, how long would it take him to tie the record?

⑩ Before going on vacation together, Mark and Eric agreed to share the expenses equally. Eric paid $54.77 for food and $78.20 for hotels. Mark paid $38.25 for gas and $39.50 for entertainment. How much does Mark owe Eric?

ANSWERS ·

① 16 pencils, $2.40
② $720 more
③ 10.24 mm
④ $12.50
⑤ 36 comic books
⑥ 72 handkerchiefs
⑦ 12 days

⑧ $8.50
⑨ 7 hours and 5 minutes
⑩ $27.61

SCORING ·

Award 16.5 points for each correct answer.

165 Genius
148–132 Gifted/Superior Intelligence
115 Higher Than Usual Intelligence
99 Average Intelligence
83 Low Average Intelligence
70 or below Very Low Intelligence

✏️ Word Problems 5

❶ Four children board a school bus. Each child has four backpacks, which they pile in the back of the bus. Four dogs sit on each backpack. Each dog has four puppies. Each dog and puppy has four legs and four toes on each leg. How many toes are on the bus?

❷ Four farm workers harvested pineapples. In the afternoon they all took a nap. One man awoke and ate 1/3 of the pineapples. A second man awoke and ate 1/3 of the remaining pineapples. A third man awoke and ate 1/3 of the remaining pineapples. A fourth man awoke and found there were 8 pineapples left. How many pineapples did the men harvest?

❸ A Cineplex has 800 seats in three theaters. In Theater 1, there are 270 seats. In Theater 2, there are 150 more seats than in Theater 3. How many seats are in Theater 2?

❹ There are three drivers in the Weiss family but only one car. Each driver drives the car 152 miles each month. How many miles will the car be driven in a year?

❺ At a tire shop, the price for four .75-meter tires for a car is $100. The shop also sells 1.5-meter tires for trucks. Assuming that the price will increase proportionally with size, what will it cost for 18 tires for a big rig?

❻ Scott buys a cup of coffee for $1.08. He pays with two silver dollar coins. The cashier gives him 8 coins in change. What could these coins be?

❼ A leaky water faucet drips 3 drops per second. Each drop is 1 1/3ml. How much water is lost in one year?

❽ Sean bought a car for $5600. He sold it to Brian for 5/6 the price he paid for it. Richard bought the car for 1/5 less than Brian paid for it. Rich sold it to Ed for 3/4 of the price he paid for it. How much did Ed spend to buy the car?

❾ A college student uses his car as a taxi service during summer vacation. His insurance during the 4-month summer vacation costs $693. Gas costs $452 a month. He charges $7 per fare. How many fares does the student need to pay his expenses and his tuition of $3280?

❿ A dog is chasing a rabbit. The rabbit has a 45-foot head start. Every time the rabbit jumps 2 feet, the dog jumps 3 feet. In how many leaps will the dog catch up with the rabbit?

ANSWERS ·

① The puppies:
4 children x 4 backpacks x 4 dogs x 4 puppies x 4 legs x 4 toes: 4096

The dogs:
4 children x 4 backpacks x 4 dogs x 4 legs x 4 toes: 1024

The children:
4 children x 2 legs x 5 toes: 40

The bus driver:
2 legs x 5 toes: 10

Total toes: 5170

② 27 pineapples

③ 340 seats

④ 5472 miles

⑤ $900

⑥ Scott's change could be 3 quarters, 3 nickels, 2 pennies or
2 quarters, 4 dimes, 2 pennies.

⑦ 126,144,000 ml, or 126,144 liters

⑧ $2800

⑨ 826 fares

⑩ 45 jumps

SCORING ·

Award 16.5 points for each correct answer.

165 Genius
148–132 Gifted/Superior Intelligence
115 Higher Than Usual Intelligence
99 Average Intelligence
83 Low Average Intelligence
70 or below Very Low Intelligence

✏ Word Problems 6

1 To improve their grades, three students were permitted to take a make-up test. Lily scored 24/60 on her first test and 32/40 on her make-up test. Ed scored 35/70 on his first test and 54/60 on his make-up test. Ella scored 27/90 on her first test and 45/50 on her make-up test. Calculate the percentage by which each student improved—which student improved the most?

2 Jim said to Chris, "If you give me one cookie, then we will have an equal number of cookies." Chris said, "If you give me one cookie, then I will have twice as many cookies as you have." How many cookies did each of the boys have?

3 The beach is 160 miles away. On the trip to the beach, the driver traveled at a constant speed of 80 miles per hour. On her drive home the driver traveled at a constant speed of 48 miles per hour. What was her average speed for the round trip?

④ A gym has bought 2-pound and 5-pound disks for the weight room. There are 14 disks in all. The weight of all the 2-pound disks is the same as the weight of the 5-pound disks. How many of each type of disks does the gym have?

⑤ Points A, B, C, D, and E are arranged in alphabetical order on a straight line. The distance from A to E is 20 inches. The distance from A to D is 15 inches. The distance from B to E is 10 inches. C is halfway between B and D. What is the distance from B to C?

⑥ A student took a test with 120 questions. He got 7 times as many answers correct as incorrect. How many answers were correct and how many were incorrect?

⑦ The distance from Bangor, Maine to Seattle, Washington is 4112 miles. On a non-stop flight from Bangor, a plane averaged 760 miles per hour. On the return flight from Seattle the plane averaged 904 miles per hour.
a. How long was each flight in minutes?
b. How much longer was the flight to Seattle than the flight to Bangor?

⑧ A machine is operated by two connecting gears. Gear A has 36 teeth, Gear B has 24 teeth. How many times must Gear B turn before Gear A makes one complete revolution?

⑨ Gina bought 7 T-shirts, paying $9.95 for each. Total sales tax was $13.07. She left the store with only $7.28 in her pocket. How much money did Gina have when she entered the store?

A N S W E R S ·

① Lily got 40% of the answers correct on the first test and 80% correct on the make-up test. She improved by 40%.

Ed got 50% of the answers correct on the first test and 90% correct on the make-up test. He improved by 40%.

Ella got 30% of the answers correct on the first test and 90% correct on the make-up test. She improved by 60%—the best of the three.

② Jim had 5 cookies, Chris had 7.

③ 60 miles per hour

④ 10 2-pound disks and 4 5-pound disks

⑤ 2.5 inches

⑥ 105 correct, 15 incorrect

⑦ a. Bangor to Seattle: 324 minutes; Seattle to Bangor: 273 minutes b. 51 minutes longer

⑧ Gear B must turn 1 1/2 times.

⑨ $90

SCORING ·

Award 16.5 points for each correct answer.

165 Genius
148–132 Gifted/Superior Intelligence
115 Higher Than Usual Intelligence
99 Average Intelligence
83 Low Average Intelligence
70 or below Very Low Intelligence

CHAPTER 2

MIXED NUMBER
QUIZZES

Euclid
(c. 322-275 BC)

Although he virtually invented the science of geometry, we know very little about Euclid. It is one of the tragedies of history that so many books and manuscripts from the ancient world have not survived. Something so simple as a library fire or as disastrous as a war has deprived us of centuries of information and wisdom.

Historians believe that Euclid taught mathematics, especially geometry, in Alexandria, one of the greatest cultural and intellectual centers of the ancient Mediterranean world. The city had been founded by Alexander the Great (who named it for himself), and at the time Euclid was teaching there, the pharaoh of Egypt was one of Alexander's generals, Ptolemy I. Although he was a king and a general, Ptolemy also had intellectual interests, including mathematics. He acquired a copy of Euclid's book, *Elements*, and began studying it, but he found it difficult to get through. It's said that when Ptolemy asked Euclid if there was a simpler way to learn geometry, Euclid, replied, "There is no royal road to geometry." In other words, there is no easy short cut to mastering this particular field of mathematics. That fact has discouraged students of geometry for centuries.

Elements is best known for teaching geometry through a series of logical steps known as proofs. These proofs are still the foundation of geometry and other areas of mathematics to this day. But there is another aspect of *Elements*: number theory, which includes the study of prime numbers and rational numbers.

Euclid's fascination with geometry led him to branch out. He studied the movement of spheres, how images are reflected on mirrors, and wrote a book on perspective, that was influential among artists during the Renaissance.

✏️ Number Series 1

1 Which number does not belong in this series?

$1 - 2 - 5 - 10 - 13 - 26 - 29 - 48$

A. 1   **B.** 5   **C.** 13   **D.** 48

2 Which number will be next in this series?

$1 - 2 - 4 - 8 - 16 - 32 -$

A. 64   **B.** 48   **C.** 40   **D.** 46

3 Which number will be next in this series?

$2 - 3 - 5 - 8 - 13 - 21 - 34 - 55 -$

A. 76   **B.** 89   **C.** 68   **D.** 75

4 Which number does not belong in this series?

$1 - 2 - 3 - 6 - 9 - 18 - 27 - 45$

A. 6   **B.** 45   **C.** 18   **D.** 27

5 Which number will be next in this series?

$3 - 9 - 27 - 81 - 243 - 729 -$

A. 1458   **B.** 810   **C.** 992   **D.** 2187

6 Which number will be next in this series?

$113 - 105 - 96 - 88 - 79 - 71 -$

A. 62   **B.** 52   **C.** 61   **D.** 63

7 What number does not belong in this series?

25 – 29 – 33 – 37 – 41 – 46

A. 33   **B.** 29   **C.** 46   **D.** 41

8 What number does not belong in this series?

5 – 10 – 15 – 30 – 35 – 40 – 45 – 95

A. 35   **B.** 40   **C.** 45   **D.** 95

9 Supply the missing numbers

– 109 –   – 95 – 88 – 81 – 74 – 67

A. 121 and 101   **C.** 116 and 103
B. 116 and 102   **D.** 117 and 102

10 Supply the missing numbers.

59 –   –   – 74 – 79 – 84 – 89

A. 62 and 67   **C.** 64 and 69
B. 64 and 68   **D.** 66 and 69

A N S W E R S ·

① D. 48 The pattern is double, then add 3.
② A. 64 The pattern is double the number.
③ B. 89 The pattern is add the previous number.
④ B. 45 The pattern is add the two previous numbers, then double.
⑤ D. 2187 The pattern is triple the previous number.
⑥ A. 62 The pattern is minus 8, then minus 9.
⑦ C. 46 The pattern is add 4.

⑧ D 95 The pattern is count by five, double the third number.
⑨ B 116 and 102 The pattern is subtract 7 from the previous number.
⑩ C 64 and 69 The pattern is add 5 to the previous number.

SCORING ·

Award 16.5 points for each correct answer.

165 Genius
148–132 Gifted/Superior Intelligence
115 Higher Than Usual Intelligence
99 Average Intelligence
83 Low Average Intelligence
70 or below Very Low Intelligence

✏️ Prime Factors 1

❶ What is the prime factorization of 16?

❷ What is the prime factorization of 180?

❸ What is the prime factorization of 196?

❹ What is the prime factorization of 36?

❺ What is the prime factorization of 24?

❻ What is the prime factorization of 18?

❼ What is the prime factorization of 225?

❽ What is the prime factorization of 63?

❾ What is the prime factorization of 75?

❿ What is the prime factorization of 50?

ANSWERS ····································

① 2^4
② $2^2 \times 3^2 \times 5$
③ $2^2 \times 7^2$
④ $2^2 \times 3^2$
⑤ $2^3 \times 3$
⑥ 2×3^2
⑦ $3^2 \times 5^2$
⑧ $3^2 \times 7$
⑨ 3×5^2
⑩ 2×5^2

SCORING ····································

Award 16.5 points for each correct answer.

165 Genius
148–132 Gifted/Superior Intelligence
115 Higher Than Usual Intelligence
99 Average Intelligence
83 Low Average Intelligence
70 or below Very Low Intelligence

✏️ Convert to Roman Numerals

Convert the following Arabic numbers to Roman numerals.

1 800

    a. MXXX
    b. DCCC
    c. CDDD
    d. XIXI

2 1066

    a. XLVI
    b. MXXXXVI
    c. DLXVI
    d. MLXVI

3 1620

    a. MDCXX
    b. DVIXX
    c. CMXX
    d. LMLL

4 333

    a. MXXX
    b. CCCXXXIII
    c. DDDXXXIII
    d. LMXXX

5 99

    a. XCIX
    b. XLIX
    c. XDIX
    d. XMIX

6 1776

    a. VIIVI
    b. DMXXVI
    c. MDCCLXXVI
    d. XVILXXVI

7 1492

    a. XIVDXCII
    b. MCDXCII
    c. CMCII
    d. DXCII

8 1984

    a. XIXLXXX
    b. XXILXXIV
    c. MCMLXXXIV
    d. LMCLXXXIV

9 55

    a. XV
    b. CV
    c. DV
    d. LV

10 2000

    a. XX
    b. LL
    c. CC
    d. MM

ANSWERS

① b. DCCC
② d. MLXVI
③ a. MDCXX
④ b. CCCXXXIII
⑤ a. XCIX
⑥ c. MDCCLXXVI
⑦ b. MCDXCII
⑧ c. MCMLXXXIV
⑨ d. LV
⑩ d. MM

SCORING

Award 16.5 points for each correct answer.

165 Genius
148–132 Gifted/Superior Intelligence
115 Higher Than Usual Intelligence
99 Average Intelligence
83 Low Average Intelligence
70 or below Very Low Intelligence

Number Series 2

Identify the next number in this series.

1 $2 - 4 - 6 - 8 - 10 - 12 - 11 - 9 - 6 -$

A. 5   **B.** 2   **C.** 4   **D.** 1

2 $4 - 8 - 12 - 20 - 32 - 52 -$

A. 84   **B.** 67   **C.** 74   **D.** 83

3 $8 - 11 - 9 - 12 - 10 - 13 -$

A. 8   **B.** 9   **C.** 10   **D.** 11

④ 540 − 538 − 535 − 533 − 530 −

    A. 525   **B.** 529   **C.** 528   **D.** 527

⑤ 1114 − 1116 − 1120 − 1126 − 1134 −

    A. 1142   **B.** 1138   **C.** 1140   **D.** 1144

⑥ 980 − 983 − 987 − 992 − 998 −

    A. 1005   **B.** 1000   **C.** 1001   **D.** 1003

⑦ 22 − 33 − 55 − 88 − 132 −

    A. 197   **B.** 187   **C.** 157   **D.** 167

⑧ 123 − 139 − 155 − 171 − 187 −

    A. 199   **B.** 189   **C.** 203   **D.** 201

⑨ 987 − 972 − 957 − 942 − 927 −

    A. 921   **B.** 915   **C.** 917   **D.** 912

⑩ 3752 − 4753 − 5755 − 6758 − 7762 −

    A. 7767   **B.** 8742   **C.** 8767   **D.** 8752

ANSWERS ·

① B. 2 The pattern is count by two, then subtract by 1, 2, 3, 4

② A. 84 The pattern is each number is the sum of the previous two numbers.

③ D. 11 The pattern is add 3, subtract 2.

④ C. 528. The pattern is subtract two, subtract 3.

⑤ D. 1144. The pattern is add by twos: plus 2, plus 4, plus 6, plus 8, etc.

⑥ A. 1005. The pattern is add 3, then 4, then 5, and so on.

⑦ B. 187. The pattern is add 11, then add 22, then 33, then 44, then 55.

⑧ C. 203. The pattern is add 16.

⑨ D. 912. The pattern is subtract 15.

⑩ C. 8767. The pattern is add 1001, 1002, 1003, 1004, 1005, etc.

SCORING ·

Award 16.5 points for each correct answer.

165 Genius
148–132 Gifted/Superior Intelligence
115 Higher Than Usual Intelligence
99 Average Intelligence
83 Low Average Intelligence
70 or below Very Low Intelligence

✏ Prime Factors 2

1 What is the prime factorization of 32?

2 What is the prime factorization of 45?

3 What is the prime factorization of 48?

4 What is the prime factorization of 56?

5 What is the prime factorization of 245?

6 What is the prime factorization of 100?

7 What is the prime factorization of 98?

8 What is the prime factorization of 525?

9 What is the prime factorization of 120?

10 What is the prime factorization of 30?

ANSWERS ·

10 $2 \times 3 \times 5$

9 $2^3 \times 3 \times 5$

8 $3 \times 5^2 \times 7$

7 2×7^2

6 $2^2 \times 5^2$

5 5×7^2

4 $2^3 \times 7$

3 $2^4 \times 3$

2 $3^2 \times 5$

1 2^5

SCORING ·

Award 16.5 points for each correct answer.

165 Genius
148–132 Gifted/Superior Intelligence
115 Higher Than Usual Intelligence
99 Average Intelligence
83 Low Average Intelligence
70 or below Very Low Intelligence

✏️ Convert to Arabic Numbers

Convert the following Roman numbers to Arabic numbers.

1 MDCCCXLVIII

    a. 1848
    b. 1958
    c. 1548
    d. 448

2 MDCXCII

    a. 1492
    b. 1592
    c. 1692
    d. 1682

3 MDCCCXC

    a. 1690
    b. 1740
    c. 1840
    d. 1890

4 MCMIX

    a. 1009
    b. 1909
    c. 1990
    d. 690

5 MCMXLI

    a. 951
    b. 1941
    c. 1451
    d. 1461

6 MCMLXIII

    a. 1963
    b. 1953
    c. 1333
    d. 33

7 MXCIII

    a. 93
    b. 903
    c. 1503
    d. 1093

8 DCCLXXVII

    a. 1707
    b. 717
    c. 777
    d. 7777

9 LIII

    a. 53
    b. 103
    c. 1003
    d. 503

10 MDXXXV

    a. 1535
    b. 555
    c. 1491
    d. 1405

ANSWERS ···

① a. 1848
② c. 1692
③ d. 1890
④ b. 1909
⑤ b. 1941

⑥ a. 1963
⑦ d. 1093
⑧ c. 777
⑨ a. 53
⑩ a. 1535

SCORING ···

Award 16.5 points for each correct answer.

165 Genius
148–132 Gifted/Superior Intelligence
115 Higher Than Usual Intelligence
99 Average Intelligence
83 Low Average Intelligence
70 or below Very Low Intelligence

CHAPTER 3

FRACTIONS

Leonardo Fibonacci
(c.1170-c.1250)

The dates of his birth and death aren't the only thing open to question regarding this mathematician; even his name is far from certain. Sometimes he appears as Leonardo Bonacci, or Leonardo Pisano, or Leonardo Pisano Bigallo, or just plain Leonardo of Pisa.

Leonardo was born into a wealthy family of Italian merchants. His father had a trading post in what is now Bejaia, Algeria. When Leonardo was a boy, his father took him to Bejaia so he could learn the family business. Young Leonardo had a head for figures, so he was very useful in a mercantile establishment. And it was in Algeria that he discovered something that would change the world.

Back home in Europe the Roman numeral system was still in force. It was awkward to use even in simple arithmetic—imagine having to add **MCLXI** and **XXXIX** (the answer, by the way, is

MCC). Roman numerals were also a stumbling block to the study of higher mathematics because the Roman system did not have zero. In Algeria, Leonardo learned about Hindu-Arabic numerals, probably from his father's Muslim merchant colleagues. Simple, efficient, and containing zero, the Hindu-Arabic system was an enormous improvement on Roman numerals. As a young man, Fibonacci traveled around the Mediterranean world, studying mathematics with the finest Arab teachers he could find. In 1200, he returned home to Italy. And two years later he published The *Book of Abacus*, or the *Book of Calculation*, that introduced the Hindu-Arabic numerals to Western Europe.

Scholars, merchants, and bankers recognized the importance of the system immediately. The Hindu-Arabic numbers simplified bookkeeping, recording weights and measures, and calculating interest, as well as opening up new possibilities in the study of mathematics.

The German emperor, Frederick II, who was interested in the sciences, read Fibonacci's book and was so impressed he invited him to be a guest in his palace. Cities in Italy competed to have him as a scholar in residence. In the end, he moved to Pisa, where the Pisans promised him not only respect and a title, but also a house and a salary.

◁═▷ Fractions 1

Multiply the following fractions.

1 $1/50 \times 1/10 =$

6 $3/11 \times 1/4 =$

2 $1/9 \times 1/8 =$

7 $3/8 \times 1/8 =$

3 $1/12 \times 1/12 =$

8 $8/9 \times 1/3 =$

4 $126/254 \times 50/61 =$

9 $7/8 \times 1/4 =$

5 $5/8 \times 7/9 =$

10 $4/8 \times 9/11 =$

A N S W E R S ·

10 9/22

5 35/72

6 7/32

4 6300/15,494

8 8/27

3 1/144

7 3/64

2 1/72

9 3/44

1 1/500

S C O R I N G ·

Award 16.5 points for each correct answer.

165 Genius
148–132 Gifted/Superior Intelligence
115 Higher Than Usual Intelligence
99 Average Intelligence
83 Low Average Intelligence
70 or below Very Low Intelligence

✏️ Fractions 2

Fill in the missing number to change the fraction to their new denominators.

1 51/256 = ___ /512

6 1/9 = ___ /18

2 4/15 = ___ /30

7 8/211 = ___ /422

3 12/18 = ___ /36

8 9/15 = ___ /30

4 5/16 = ___ /32

9 15/31 = ___ /62

5 9/11 = ___ /44

10 81/1024 = ___ /4096

ANSWERS ·

10 324/4096

5 36/44

9 30/62

4 10/32

8 18/30

3 24/36

7 16/422

2 8/30

6 2/18

1 102/512

SCORING ·

Award 16.5 points for each correct answer.

165 Genius
148–132 Gifted/Superior Intelligence
115 Higher Than Usual Intelligence
99 Average Intelligence
83 Low Average Intelligence
70 or below Very Low Intelligence

✏️ Fractions 3

Divide the following fractions.

1 $1/3 \div 1/9 =$

6 $3/8 \div 3 =$

2 $16/31 \div 8/81 =$

7 $51/60 \div 14/120 =$

3 $1/4 \div 8/1 =$

8 $7/8 \div 5/8 =$

4 $3/4 \div 1/16 =$

9 $7/8 \div 8 =$

5 $3/8 \div 1/16 =$

10 $88/256 \div 411/512 =$

ANSWERS ·

10 45,056/105,216 or 176/411

5 48/8 or 6

6 1/32

4 48/4 or 12

8 56/40 or 1 2/5

3 1/32

7 6120/840 or 7 2/7

2 1296/248 or 5 7/31

9 3/24 or 1/8

1 9/3 or 3

SCORING ·

Award 16.5 points for each correct answer.

165 Genius
148–132 Gifted/Superior Intelligence
115 Higher Than Usual Intelligence
99 Average Intelligence
83 Low Average Intelligence
70 or below Very Low Intelligence

✏️ Fractions 4

Reduce the fractions to the lowest terms.

1 12/18

6 18/27

2 6/20

7 18/36

3 5/30

8 55/66

4 10/14

9 12/14

5 6/16

10 8/14

ANSWERS ·

10 4/7

5 3/8

9 6/7

4 5/7

8 5/6

3 1/6

7 1/2

2 3/10

6 2/3

1 2/3

SCORING ·

Award 16.5 points for each correct answer.

165 Genius
148–132 Gifted/Superior Intelligence
115 Higher Than Usual Intelligence
99 Average Intelligence
83 Low Average Intelligence
70 or below Very Low Intelligence

✏️ Fractions 5

Multiply the following mixed numbers.
Example: 1 1/3 x 2 = 4/3 x 2/1 = 8/3 or 2 2/3

1 3 1/8 x 1/2 =   x   =   **6** 6 4/5 x 1 1/2 =   x   =

2 3 2/3 x 1/4 =   x   =   **7** 2 1/6 x 1/3 =   x   =

3 4 1/3 x 2 1/2 =   x   =   **8** 2 x 3 1/3 =   x   =

4 2 1/2 x 2 1/2 =   x   =   **9** 15 1/2 x 15 1/2 =   x   =

5 4 1/8 x 4 1/8 =   x   =   **10** 6 1/5 x 1/3 =   x   =

A N S W E R S ·

10 31/15 or 2 1/15   **5** 1089/64 or 17 1/64

6 961/4 or 240 1/4   **4** 25/4 or 6 1/4

8 14/2 or 6 2/3   **3** 65/6 or 10 5/6

7 13/18   **2** 11/12

9 102/10 or 10 1/5   **1** 25/16 or 1 9/16

S C O R I N G ·

Award 16.5 points for each correct answer.

165 Genius
148–132 Gifted/Superior Intelligence
115 Higher Than Usual Intelligence
99 Average Intelligence
83 Low Average Intelligence
70 or below Very Low Intelligence

✏️ Fractions to Percent

Convert the following fractions to percent.

1 5/8

6 9/90

2 11/16

7 13/33

3 1/12

8 17/21

4 4/20

9 23/58

5 6/19

10 2/9

ANSWERS ·

10 22.22%

5 31.57%

6 39.65%

4 20%

8 80.95%

3 8.3%

7 39.39%

2 68.75%

9 10%

1 62.5%

SCORING ·

Award 16.5 points for each correct answer.

165 Genius
148–132 Gifted/Superior Intelligence
115 Higher Than Usual Intelligence
99 Average Intelligence
83 Low Average Intelligence
70 or below Very Low Intelligence

CHAPTER 4

DECIMALS

Rene Descartes
(1596-1650)

Rene Descartes is famous for that pithy philosophical maxim, "I think, therefore I am." The human mind fascinated him, leading him to believe that rational thought was absolutely an essential part of what makes us human. But he wasn't all brain and no heart—Descartes also wrote a book entitled *Passions of the Soul*, which explored human emotions.

The 17th century was a golden age for philosophical exploration and advances in the sciences. The philosophers John Locke, Jean-Jacques Rousseau, and David Hume were active at this time; so were Galileo, Isaac Newton, and Anton van Leeuwenhoek, the inventor of the microscope. But Descartes came late to the philosophy-and-sciences party. As a young man he fought as a mercenary for the Dutch in their war against Spain. He said later that it was a series of three vivid dreams that convinced him to give up soldiering and pursue wisdom.

Although a Frenchman, he settled comfortably in the Netherlands, where he lived off a fortune he had made in the bond market. With no need to work for a living, he had plenty of leisure time to devote to study and writing. His most famous philosophical work is *Discourse on Method*, in which he lays out a set of principles for discerning what is true.

In mathematics, Descartes gave us the Cartesian coordinates system, which shows how algebraic equations can be represented as geometric shapes. He also invented analytic geometry.

In his final years, Descartes moved to Sweden to tutor Queen Christina. This splendidly robust young woman liked to study very early in the morning. Traveling to the palace before dawn in a bitter Swedish winter, Descartes caught pneumonia; several days later he died.

✏️ Decimals 1

Add the following decimals.

1. $8.95 + 1.90 =$

2. $44.91 + .20 =$

3. $1.5 + 2.5 =$

4. $9.09 + .2 =$

5. $.3 + 1.55 =$

6. $4.4 + 8.8 =$

7. $16.00 + 1.05 =$

8. $9.99 + 100.99 =$

9. $11.43 + 17.17 =$

10. $107.09 + 239.17 =$

A N S W E R S ·

10. 346.26

9. 28.60

8. 110.98

7. 17.05

6. 13.2

5. 1.85

4. 9.29

3. 4

2. 45.11

1. 10.85

S C O R I N G ·

Award 16.5 points for each correct answer.

165 Genius
148–132 Gifted/Superior Intelligence
115 Higher Than Usual Intelligence
99 Average Intelligence
83 Low Average Intelligence
70 or below Very Low Intelligence

✏️ Decimals 2

Subtract the following decimals.

1 23.06 – 14.07 =

6 14.4 – 13.9 =

2 1.44 - .6 =

7 6.66 – 4.48 =

3 9.31 – 1.2 =

8 29 – 1.4 =

4 16.23 – 1.4 =

9 18.1 – 1.44 =

5 144.2 – 128.3 =

10 .228 - .01 =

ANSWERS ·

10 .218

9 16.66

8 27.6

7 2.18

6 .5

5 15.9

4 14.83

3 8.11

2 .84

1 8.99

SCORING ·

Award 16.5 points for each correct answer.

165 Genius
148–132 Gifted/Superior Intelligence
115 Higher Than Usual Intelligence
99 Average Intelligence
83 Low Average Intelligence
70 or below Very Low Intelligence

Decimals 3

Multiply the following decimals.

1   1.2
   x 2.4

6   11.22
   x .4

2   3.11
   x 2.4

7   .44
   x 6.0

3   18.2
   x 1.1

8   .49
   x .06

4   1.2
   x 9.0

9   4.44
   x 1.6

5   8.6
   x 4.4

10   .12
   x .06

ANSWERS ·

10 .0072

5 37.84

6 7.104

4 10.8

8 .0294

3 20.02

7 2.64

2 7.464

9 4.488

1 2.88

SCORING ·

Award 16.5 points for each correct answer.

165 Genius
148–132 Gifted/Superior Intelligence
115 Higher Than Usual Intelligence
99 Average Intelligence
83 Low Average Intelligence
70 or below Very Low Intelligence

◁▷ Decimals 4

Divide the following decimals.

1 $4.5 \div 1.8 =$ **6** $1.88 \div .04 =$

2 $5.5 \div 1.1 =$ **7** $.440 \div 8.8 =$

3 $8.4 \div 2.4 =$ **8** $15.3 \div 4.7 =$

4 $5.0 \div 4.0 =$ **9** $.967 \div .47 =$

5 $15.5 \div 2.0 =$ **10** $11.13 \div 2.73 =$

ANSWERS ·

10 4.08   **5** 7.75
9 2.05   **4** 1.25
8 3.25   **3** 3.5
7 .05   **2** 5.0
6 47.0   **1** 2.5

SCORING ··

Award 16.5 points for each correct answer.

165 Genius
148–132 Gifted/Superior Intelligence
115 Higher Than Usual Intelligence
99 Average Intelligence
83 Low Average Intelligence
70 or below Very Low Intelligence

✐ Decimals 5

Convert the following decimals to fractions.

1. 4.17

2. 2.5

3. 9.1

4. 21.6

5. 9.123

6. 33.8

7. 41.3

8. 50.7

9. 7.8

10. 12.6

ANSWERS ···

⑩ 12 3/5

⑨ 7 4/5

⑧ 50 7/10

⑦ 41 3/10

⑥ 33 4/5

⑤ 9 123/1000

④ 21 3/5

③ 9 1/10

② 2 1/2

① 4 17/100

SCORING

Award 16.5 points for each correct answer.

165 Genius
148–132 Gifted/Superior Intelligence
115 Higher Than Usual Intelligence
99 Average Intelligence
83 Low Average Intelligence
70 or below Very Low Intelligence

✏️ Decimals 6

Convert the following decimals to percents.

1. .65

2. .125

3. 4.5

4. 78.9

5. .045

6. 3.24

7. 11.34

8. 9.09

9. 4.006

10. .0567

ANSWERS

① 65%
② 12.5%
③ 450%
④ 7890%
⑤ 4.5%
⑥ 324%
⑦ 1134%
⑧ 909%
⑨ 400.6%
⑩ 5.67%

SCORING ·

Award 16.5 points for each correct answer.

165 Genius
148–132 Gifted/Superior Intelligence
115 Higher Than Usual Intelligence
99 Average Intelligence
83 Low Average Intelligence
70 or below Very Low Intelligence

CHAPTER 5

MORE WORD
PROBLEMS

Isaac Newton
(1642-1727)

When you look up the word "genius" in the dictionary, the definition ought to be accompanied by a portrait of Isaac Newton. His lifetime saw a flowering of interest in the sciences, but Newton's discoveries actually advanced mathematics and science. He is called "the Father of Calculus" (although he called it fluxions). He expanded the fields of analytic geometry, algebra, trigonometry, and the theory of equations.

When he wasn't working in mathematics, Newton studied optics, thermodynamics, acoustics, and astronomy. It was Newton who described accurately for the very first time in human history the motion of the planets. His Three Laws of Motion are basic in any physics class, as is his Law of Gravitation. It's said that one day, as Newton was sitting in the shade of an apple tree, an apple came loose and beaned him. That incident is supposed to have inspired Newton to study gravity. The falling apple story may or may not be true, but Newton's conclusions regarding the laws of gravity were groundbreaking. Newton was also the first person to notice that when light passes through a crystal prism, the entire spectrum of colors is revealed.

But Newton was more than a full-time brainiac; he had a playful side too. As a young man he built a miniature windmill and powered it with a mouse that ran on a treadmill.

Late in life Newton was elected to Parliament, but his genius did not shine among the career politicians. It is said that he felt so out of his element, that he never said a word in the parliamentary debates. According to legend, he spoke up only once—when he complained of a draft and asked that a window be shut.

During his final years, Newton kept a strange secret: the greatest living scientist, arguably the greatest scientist who ever lived, became obsessed with alchemy, a kind of pseudo-science that combined magic with a healthy dollop of wishful thinking. It hurts to think that the brilliant Isaac Newton squandered years of his life trying to change lead into silver and copper into gold.

At his death, Newton was buried among the monarchs and notables of England in Westminster Abbey. The epitaph on his tombstone reads, "Let mortals rejoice that so great an ornament to the human race has existed."

✏️ More Word Problems 1

1. By using plus signs and minus signs, arrange the numbers so the answer will be 100. You may group the numbers to make a larger numeral, such as 123, but you may not change the order of the numbers. 123456789 = 100

2. There are 24 girls who swim on the Mako Sharks swim team. There are 27 girls who swim on the Mighty Ducks swim team. The Flying Tunas have 18 fewer swimmers on their team than on the Makos and the Ducks combined. How many girls swim for the Flying Tunas?

3. Joey and Lisa entered an 8-mile walkathon for a local charity. Joey's 12 sponsors pledged $4 per mile. Lisa's 18 sponsors pledged $2 per mile. Joey and Lisa both completed the course. How much more money did Joey make than Lisa?

4. On his last four math tests, Adam has scored 73, 85, 81, and 71. There is one test to go in the semester. If Adam's scores for the five tests total 400, he will have an average score of 80. What score must Adam get on the fifth math test to achieve an 80 average?

5. The horror movie playing in Cinema 1 is 90 minutes long. The romantic comedy playing in Cinema 2 is 2 hours long. What is the ratio of the length of the two movies?

6. Jason bought a new stereo system. He made a deposit of $25 and agreed to pay $15 per month for the next two years. What was the cost of the stereo system?

7. At a discount store, Ed bought a DVD and a CD. The total cost was $20. The DVD cost $10 more than the CD. What was the cost of each item?

⑧ Maura has started walking for exercise. The first week she walked 1 mile. The second week she walked 5 miles. The third week she walked 9 miles. The fourth week she walked 13 miles. The fifth week she walked 17 miles. If this pattern of increases continues at the same rate, in what week will Maura walk 37 miles?

⑨ Aaron works 12 hours a week at a pizzeria. He can divide his hours over three days, but he must spend at least three hours at work on any given day—and working a part of an hour doesn't count. In how many ways can Aaron split up his hours over the three days?

⑩ Liam goes to the movies. He buys one ticket and a small popcorn. The total cost is $11. The ticket cost $5 more than the popcorn. How much did the ticket cost?

ANSWERS ·

① There are eleven ways to solve this problem.

$123 + 45 - 67 + 8 - 9 = 100$
$123 + 4 - 5 + 67 - 89 = 100$
$123 - 45 - 67 + 89 = 100$
$123 - 4 - 5 - 6 - 7 + 8 - 9 = 100$
$12 + 3 + 4 + 5 - 6 - 7 + 89 = 100$
$12 + 3 - 4 + 5 + 67 + 8 + 9 = 100$
$12 - 3 - 4 + 5 - 6 + 7 + 89 = 100$
$1 + 23 - 4 + 56 + 7 + 8 + 9 = 100$
$1 + 23 - 4 + 5 + 6 + 78 - 9 = 100$
$1 + 2 + 34 - 5 + 67 - 8 + 9 = 100$
$1 + 2 + 3 - 4 + 5 + 6 + 78 + 9 = 100$

② 33 girls swim for the Flying Tunas.

③ Joey collected $96 more than Lisa.

④ Adam needs 90 points on the fifth test.

⑤ 3 to 4

⑥ $385

⑦ $15 for the DVD, $5 for the CD

⑧ The tenth week

⑨ There are 10 different ways Aaron can arrange his schedule.

⑩ The movie ticket cost $8.

SCORING ·

Award 16.5 points for each correct answer.

165 Genius
148–132 Gifted/Superior Intelligence
115 Higher Than Usual Intelligence
99 Average Intelligence
83 Low Average Intelligence
70 or below Very Low Intelligence

✏ More Word Problems 2

① A coffee shop pays its employees $7.95 per hour Monday through Friday and $9.25 per hour Saturday and Sunday. Starting on a Monday, Dave worked seven hours per day for six consecutive days. How much did he earn?

② Each chocolate chip cookie in a package measures 1.75 inches in diameter. How many cookies will it take to create a line one-yard long? Round off your answer to the nearest whole number.

③ A local marathon covers a distance of 26.2 miles. Convert the distance to kilometers, with 1 mile equal to 1.6 kilometers.

④ A local phone call costs 35 cents per minute for the first three minutes, and 25 cents per minute for each minute thereafter. Tyler made a phone call for which he was charged $1.85. How many minutes was Tyler on the phone?

⑤ Human hair grows an average of .013 inch per day. How many inches long would your hair be if you did not cut it for three non-leap years? Round off your answer to the nearest hundredth.

⑥ Sam brought 7 liters of juice to a barbecue. Ellen brought 3 gallons of juice. Sam said that he had brought more juice. Calculate if Sam is correct, assuming that 1 liter equals .26 gallons.

⑦ For his birthday Paul received $100. He wants to buy two magazine racks that cost $15.95 each, a CD rack which costs $49.75, and one mouse pad that costs $7.89. Shipping for orders that total $76 to $99.99 is $11.95. Is Paul's $100 enough to cover the costs of the items and the shipping? If not, how much more will he need?

⑧ Alex ran 35 miles last week. He ran 40 miles this week. What is the ratio of miles from last week to this week?

⑨ Mariah is baking a cake that calls for 2 1/4 cups of flour, 3/4 cup of white sugar, and 1 1/2 cups of brown sugar. Mariah decides to double the recipe. How many cups of each ingredient will she need?

⑩ On Monday when the stock exchange opened, one share of Big Value stock was valued at 15.5 points. When the market closed at the end of the day Tuesday, Big Value stock had increased in value by 1.75 points. How much was a single share of stock worth now?

ANSWERS ·

① $343

② 21 cookies

③ 41.92 kilometers

④ 9 minutes

⑤ 14.24 inches

⑥ Sam's 7 liters equal 1.82 gallons.

⑦ $1.49

⑧ 7 to 8

⑨ 4 1/2 cups of flour; 1 1/2 cups of white sugar; 3 cups of brown sugar.

⑩ 17.25 points

SCORING ··

Award 16.5 points for each correct answer.

165 Genius
148–132 Gifted/Superior Intelligence
115 Higher Than Usual Intelligence
99 Average Intelligence
83 Low Average Intelligence
70 or below Very Low Intelligence

✏️ More Word Problems 3

1. On a visit to New York City, Megan walked 3 2/3 miles to the Empire State Building, 2 4/5 miles to the Metropolitan Museum of Art, and 5 5/6 miles to Times Square. How many miles did Megan walk in New York?

2. Lizzie has a box filled with beads. Each bead is 3/4 of an inch long. She wants to make a 12-inch necklace. How many beads will she need?

3. A cookie recipe for 36 cookies calls for 1/3 cup of butter, 2 1/2 cups of flour, and 3/4 cup of sugar. Lenny wants to make 48 cookies. Calculate the total cups of ingredients he will need to make 48 cookies.

4. Drew's after tax take-home pay is $840. He budgets 1/10 for savings, 2/7 for rent, 1/5 for his car loan, 1/6 for utilities. How much is left of Drew's salary?

5. Assuming that a foot equals 3/10 of a meter, calculate the length in meters of 100-foot-long football field.

6. Express as a fraction one minute of one day.

7. In one season, the Stingers soccer team won 15 games and lost 25 games. What is the ratio of games won to games lost?

8. Three students were each given 24 tickets to sell for a school play. Lisa sold 2/3 of her tickets. Mark sold 1/4 of his tickets. Melanie sold 5/12 of her tickets. How many tickets did each student sell?

9. A parking garage charges $6 for the first hour and $5 for each additional hour or part of an hour. Emily parked her car at 1 pm and picked it up at 5:30 pm. What will she be charged?

10. A pair of running shoes costs $70. A pair of cross trainers costs $84. What is the ratio of the price of the two types of shoes?

ANSWERS

1. 12 3/10 miles
2. 16 beads
3. 4 7/9 cups of ingredients
4. $208
5. 30 meters
6. 1/1440
7. 3 to 5
8. Lisa sold 16 tickets; Mark sold 6 tickets; Melanie sold 10 tickets.
9. $26
10. 5 to 6

SCORING

Award 16.5 points for each correct answer.

165 Genius
148–132 Gifted/Superior Intelligence
115 Higher Than Usual Intelligence

99 Average Intelligence
83 Low Average Intelligence
70 or below Very Low Intelligence

✏️ More Word Problems 4

1 A diner sold 75 breakfast specials between 7:30 am and 8 am. It sold 100 breakfast specials between 8 am and 8:30 am. What is the ratio of the breakfast specials during those two time periods?

2 A fruit and vegetable stand is selling 5 pounds of green beans for $2.55. At this rate, what is the cost of 1 pound of green beans?

3 Steven bought 8 six-packs of soda for a party. The party had 16 guests. Steve gave each guest the same number of cans. How many cans of soda did each guest receive?

4 Travis drove 510 miles in 8.5 hours. How many miles did he cover per hour?

5 A pizzeria has a children's menu. Children under age 12 can have one slice of pizza for $1.25 and one ice cream cone for 45 cents. What is the ratio of the price for the slice of pizza to the price of the ice cream cone?

6 Alice ran 3/4 of a cross-country race in 18 minutes. Assuming that she can keep up this pace, in how many minutes will Alice complete the course?

7 As a prank, a group of college students mounted a bathtub on wheels and pushed it 320 miles in 24 hours. Assuming that they pushed the tub at a consistent rate every hour, how many miles did they push the tub in 6 hours?

8 A standard pasta bowl weighs 2 ounces. The largest pasta bowl ever made weighed 605 pounds. What is the ratio of the two pasta bowls?

9 A car wash offers its customers three options: six coupons for $33, two washes for $11.50, and one wash for $5.95. Which is the least expensive option?

10 Professor Andrews arranged 28 history books side by side on a bookshelf. The books measured 42 inches long. How many books can be arranged on the shelf per foot?

ANSWERS ·

① 3 to 4
② 51 cents
③ 3 cans
④ 60 miles per hour
⑤ 25 to 9
⑥ 6 minutes
⑦ 80 miles in 6 hours
⑧ 1 to 4840
⑨ The coupons offer car washes for $5.50 each.
⑩ 8 books per foot

SCORING ·

Award 16.5 points for each correct answer.

165 Genius
148–132 Gifted/Superior Intelligence
115 Higher Than Usual Intelligence
99 Average Intelligence
83 Low Average Intelligence
70 or below Very Low Intelligence

✏️ More Word Problems 5

1. A college summer school offers a science class that meets 5 hours a day, 5 days a week, for 2 weeks. During the fall semester the same science course meets 2 hours a day, 1 day a week, for 10 weeks. What is the ratio of the total hours of the two courses?

2. To set a world record, a barber shaved 278 men in 60 minutes. How many men did he shave in 1 minute?

3. Mia works 7 hours per day, Monday through Thursday. She earned $333. How much does Mia earn per hour?

4. A class of fourth graders read 243 books in 4.5 weeks. How many books did they read per week?

5. In New Jersey, a tax of 84 cents is added onto a $14 purchase. What is the tax rate per dollar in New Jersey?

6. Boyd runs 1.5 miles in 15 minutes, then walks 2 miles in 30 minutes. In speed, what is the difference between his hourly rate for running and his hourly rate for walking?

7. Two supermarkets are offering a sale on apples. Supermarket A is selling 4 pounds of apples for $2.36. Supermarket B is selling 6 pounds of apples for $3.54. Which is a better buy?

8. A 60-foot-high house casts a shadow 45 feet long. Next to the house stands an 8-foot-high flagpole. How long is the flagpole's shadow?

9. The key on a map of Utah says that 2 inches on the map equals 100 miles. If the distance on map between two cities is five inches, what is the distance in miles?

⑩ There are 140 students in a high school lecture hall. The ratio of boys to girls is 3 to 4. How many girls are in the lecture hall?

ANSWERS ·

① 5 to 2

② 4.63 men

③ $11.90 per hour

④ 54 books per week

⑤ 6 cents per dollar

⑥ 6 miles per hour running, 4 miles per hour walking, so the difference is 2 miles per hour

⑦ Neither store. Both are selling apples for 59 cents per pound.

⑧ 6 feet long

⑨ 250 miles

⑩ 80 girls

SCORING ·

Award 16.5 points for each correct answer.

165 Genius
148–132 Gifted/Superior Intelligence
115 Higher Than Usual Intelligence

99 Average Intelligence
83 Low Average Intelligence
70 or below Very Low Intelligence

✏️ More Word Problems 6

1. At a summer camp there are 3 counselors for every 20 campers. If there are 36 counselors, how many campers are there?

2. On a map of Iowa, 3 inches equals 25 miles. The distance between two towns is 81.25 miles. How many inches is that distance on the map?

3. A Little League slugger has been at bat 60 times and had 24 hits. How many hits will he have after 100 times at bat?

4. A CD cost $12. The sales tax is 60 cents. What will be the sales tax on a CD set that costs $20?

5. The ratio of bagels to donuts sold at a bakery is 5 to 2. In a single day 120 donuts were sold. Calculate the total number of bagels and donuts sold that day.

6. A 36-foot-high tree casts a 27-foot shadow. Sally casts a shadow that is 3-feet-long. How tall is Sally?

7. Molly is 2 times plus 4 years older than Anna. If Molly is 16 years old, how old is Anna?

8. 54 is the sum of an even number and the consecutive even number. What are the two numbers that when added together total 54?

⑨ There are 491 students at Franklin School—5 less than four times the number of students at Jefferson School. How many students are at Jefferson School?

⑩ Sam has spent $11 on a movie ticket and a box of popcorn. The popcorn cost $5 less than a ticket. How much did Sam pay for his ticket?

ANSWERS ·

① 240 campers
② 9.75 inches
③ 40 hits
④ $1
⑤ 420
⑥ 4 feet tall
⑦ 6 years old
⑧ 26 and 28
⑨ 124 students
⑩ $8

SCORING ·

Award 16.5 points for each correct answer.

165 Genius
148–132 Gifted/Superior Intelligence
115 Higher Than Usual Intelligence
99 Average Intelligence
83 Low Average Intelligence
70 or below Very Low Intelligence

CHAPTER 6

PERCENTAGE
PROBLEMS

Leonhard Euler
(1708-1783)

Growing up in Riehen, Switzerland, Leonhard Euler's family
was friends with Johann Bernoulli and his family. Bernoulli was
respected as the most distinguished mathematician in Europe.
When he found that young Leonhard had a genius for math, he
volunteered to tutor the boy. Leonhard's father hoped Leonhard
would become a Calvinist pastor, but Bernoulli persuaded his
friend that the boy was a born mathematician.

Euler moved quickly through the University of Basel. At age 19
he received his doctorate. At age 20 he entered the Paris Academy's
competition. Every year the academy proposed some scientific
problem and welcomed solutions from all comers. The problem in
1727: where was the best place to erect a mast on a ship? Euler's

solution took second place, but the next time he entered the competition, he won. In fact, he won the Paris Academy prize twelve times over the course of his life.

At the university Euler had also studied physics. In 1726, there was an opening for a physicist at the Imperial Russian Academy of Sciences in St. Petersburg. One of Bernoulli's sons taught at the academy, and he recommended Euler for the post. There were some students at the academy, but not many—the faculty wanted time for research. Euler remained at the academy until 1741, when Frederick the Great invited him to join the faculty of the Berlin Academy. During his twenty-five years at the Berlin Academy, Euler did some of his most significant work in the fields of differential calculus, infinitesimal calculus, and graph theory.

In 1766, Empress Catherine the Great lured Euler back to the academy in St. Petersburg. On September 18, 1783, Euler had lunch with his family and a colleague, Anders Johan Lexell. After the meal Euler and Lexell were chatting about the discovery of a new planet, Uranus, when Euler suffered a brain hemorrhage. Several hours later, Leonhard Euler died.

✏️ Percentage Problems 1

1 8 is what percent of 20?

2 18 is 40% of what number?

3 What is 20% of 45?

4 What is 25% of 52?

5 14 is what percent of 56?

6 18 is 75% of what number?

7 What is 15% of 200?

8 476 is 85% of what number?

9 75% of 120 is what number?

10 15 is what percent of 300?

ANSWERS ·

10 5%

9 90

8 560

7 30

6 24

5 25%

4 13

3 9

2 45

1 40%

SCORING ·

Award 16.5 points for each correct answer.

165 Genius
148–132 Gifted/Superior Intelligence
115 Higher Than Usual Intelligence
99 Average Intelligence
83 Low Average Intelligence
70 or below Very Low Intelligence

✏️ Percentage Problems 2

1. 40% of 164 is what number?

2. 90 is 75% of what number?

3. 44 is what percent of 132?

4. What is 85% of 600?

5. 1.5 is what percent of 3?

6. What is 50% of .01?

7. 1/3 is what percent of 2/3?

8. What is 5% of 34?

9. 17 is what percent of 51?

10. What is 50% of 188?

ANSWERS ·

10. 94

9. 33.3

8. 1.7

7. 50%

6. .005

5. 50%

4. 510

3. 33.3

2. 120

1. 65.6

SCORING ·

Award 16.5 points for each correct answer.

165 Genius
148–132 Gifted/Superior Intelligence
115 Higher Than Usual Intelligence
99 Average Intelligence
83 Low Average Intelligence
70 or below Very Low Intelligence

✏ Percentage Problems 3

1 What is 30% of 30?

2 What is 150% of 60?

3 What is 50% of 15?

4 7 is 80% of what number?

5 20% of what number is 40?

6 What is 15% of 1023?

7 What is 23% of 78?

8 27 is what percent of 150?

9 41 is what percent of 253?

10 9 is what percent of 11?

ANSWERS ·

10 81.81%

6 16.20%

8 18%

7 17.94

9 153.45

5 200

4 56

3 7.5

2 90

1 9

SCORING ·

Award 16.5 points for each correct answer.

165 Genius
148–132 Gifted/Superior Intelligence
115 Higher Than Usual Intelligence
99 Average Intelligence
83 Low Average Intelligence
70 or below Very Low Intelligence

✏️ Percentage Problems 4

① A clothing store is having a 25% off sale. You find a sweater you like. The original price is $120. You have a coupon for an additional 10% off.
A. How much will you pay for the sweater?
B. In dollars, how much did you save?
C. In percent, how much did you save?

② What is 43% of 12?

③ Between 2010 and 2011, sales in the housing market decreased by 28%. Between 2011 and 2012, sales in the housing market increased by 106%. What was the percent change from 2010 to 2012?

④ 57 is what percent of 422?

⑤ The butcher is having a 25% off sale. You pay $22.50 for a package of three steaks. What was the original price?

⑥ 77 is 39% of what number?

⑦ According to a census, the population of New York Metropolitan Area in 2000 was 35,306,000. Between 1990 and 2000, the population had grown by 57.9%. What was the population in 1990?

⑧ What is 71% of 971?

ANSWERS ····································

8) 689.41   4) 13.507%

7) 22,359.721   3) 48.2%

6) 197.435   2) 5.16

5) $30   1) A. $81 B. $39 C. 32.5%

SCORING ····································

Award 16.5 points for each correct answer.

165 Genius
148–132 Gifted/Superior Intelligence
115 Higher Than Usual Intelligence
99 Average Intelligence
83 Low Average Intelligence
70 or below Very Low Intelligence

✏️ Percentage Problems 5

1. What is 67 percent as a decimal?

2. What is 44% as a fraction?

3. Convert the fraction 11/12 into a percentage.

4. 13 is 14% of what number?

5. 6 is what percent of 91?

6. What is 21% of 88?

7. What is 24% as a fraction?

8. What is 1124% as a decimal?

9. What is the percentage change when 62 becomes 79?

10. What is 43% of 343?

ANSWERS ·

⑩ 147.49

⑨ 27.419%

⑧ 11.24

⑦ 6/25

⑥ 18.48

⑤ 6.593%

④ 92,857

③ 91.666%

② 11/25

① .67

SCORING ·

Award 16.5 points for each correct answer.

165 Genius
148–132 Gifted/Superior Intelligence
115 Higher Than Usual Intelligence
99 Average Intelligence
83 Low Average Intelligence
70 or below Very Low Intelligence

✎ Percentage Problems 6

① A dentist's gross salary was $189,000. His tax rate was 23%. How much did he pay in taxes?

② Alice sells online ads. She is paid a 20% commission. Her commissions last year totaled $24,000. How much ad revenue did she generate?

③ A real estate agent sold a house for $85,000. Her commission is 3% of the sale price. How much did she make on this sale?

④ Shoes are on sale at 40% off the original price. If a pair of shoes originally cost $60, how much do they cost now?

5 One pencil costs 60 cents. How much will it cost after the 5% sales tax is added?

6 There are 2100 students at a high school. 85% say gym is their favorite class. How many students love gym?

7 A grocer sold 40% of his apples. He has 420 apples left. How many apples did he originally have?

8 In an election, 7500 votes were cast. Some of the votes were valid, and some were invalid. One candidate received 55% of the valid votes and 20% of the invalid votes. What is the number (not the percent) of valid votes the other candidate received?

9 The combined weekly salary of two landscapers is $550. One landscaper's salary is equal to 120% of his co-worker's salary. How much does the other landscaper receive?

10 In a decade, a city's population increased from 175,000 to 262,500. What was the average increase per year?

ANSWERS ·

5 63 cents

6 $36

7 $2550

8 $120,000

9 $43,470

10 5%

9 $250

8 2700 votes

7 700 apple

6 1785

SCORING ·

Award 16.5 points for each correct answer.

165 Genius
148–132 Gifted/Superior Intelligence
115 Higher Than Usual Intelligence
99 Average Intelligence
83 Low Average Intelligence
70 or below Very Low Intelligence

CHAPTER 7

NEGATIVE
NUMBERS

Carl Friedrich Gauss
(1777-1855)

Carl Friedrich Gauss' father was an ordinary laborer and his mother could not read or write. Carl, on the other hand, was an intellectual prodigy who made momentous discoveries in mathematics while he was still a teenager. He described his discoveries in a book, *Disquisitiones Arithmeticae*, which is Latin for "Number Research." In his book young Carl described a new field of math, known today as algebraic number theory. It is considered a classic, and is still used in college classrooms.

Stories about the brilliant boy from a working class family reached the Duke of Braunschweig, who offered to finance Carl's education. The duke paid Carl's tuition and other expenses for the next six years.

While at the University of Gottingen, Gauss made remarkable discoveries regarding the construction of polygons, or multi-sided figures. His particular favorite was the heptadecagon, a polygon with seventeen sides.

While still an undergraduate he made more discoveries regarding prime numbers and positive integers. In 1799 he received his doctorate, and two years later, at age 23, he finally published *Disquisitiones Arithmeticae*, the book he had written when he was a teenager.

Gauss spent the rest of his life as a university professor and researcher. Some of the finest German mathematicians of the 19th century were his students, including G.F. Bernhard Riemann, who you will meet in the next chapter. He spent most of his career studying number theory and it is believed that Gauss invented a new field of mathematics, non-Euclidian geometry. He was also involved in the technological discoveries of his age, including magnetism and electrical circuits.

Towards the end of his life Gauss visited a stonecutter and asked him to prepare his tombstone. In place of a cross (Gauss was not religious), he asked that a heptadecagon be carved on his headstone. The stonecutter had no idea what such a shape looked like, and when Gauss showed him, the man turned down the job—it was just too hard to replicate.

✏️ Adding and Subtracting Negative Numbers

1 $+8 - 10 =$

6 $25 - (-4) =$

2 $-3 - 4 =$

7 $4 - (-3) =$

3 $-7 + 15 =$

8 $-8 - (-3) =$

4 $6 - (-3) =$

9 $-5 - (-3) =$

5 $5 + (-2) =$

10 $-8 + 5 =$

ANSWERS ·

① -2   ⑥ 29
② -7   ⑦ 7
③ +8   ⑧ -5
④ +9   ⑨ -2
⑤ 3   ⑩ -3

SCORING ·

Award 16.5 points for each correct answer.

165 Genius
148–132 Gifted/Superior Intelligence
115 Higher Than Usual Intelligence
99 Average Intelligence
83 Low Average Intelligence
70 or below Very Low Intelligence

✏️ Multiplying Negative Numbers

1 +5 x -2 =

2 +3 x -4 =

3 -8 x -8 =

4 -6 x +4 =

5 +6 x (-3) =

6 -9 x (-8) =

7 -7 x (+3) =

8 (-5) x (-4) =

9 -5 x -5 =

10 -5 x +5 =

ANSWERS ·

⑩ -25

⑨ +25

⑧ +20

⑦ -21

⑥ +72

⑤ -18

④ -24

③ +64

② -12

① -10

SCORING ·

Award 16.5 points for each correct answer.

165 Genius
148–132 Gifted/Superior Intelligence
115 Higher Than Usual Intelligence
99 Average Intelligence
83 Low Average Intelligence
70 or below Very Low Intelligence

Adding and Subtracting Negative Numbers 2

1 -44 + 16 =

6 98 − (-23) =

2 -36 − 20 =

7 65 + (-23) =

3 -42 + (-44) =

8 90 + (-11) =

4 39 − (-22) =

9 46 + (-98) =

5 (-36) + 21 =

10 -61 + 31 =

ANSWERS ·

10 -30

5 -15

9 -52

4 61

8 79

3 -86

7 42

2 -56

6 121

1 -28

SCORING ·

Award 16.5 points for each correct answer.

165 Genius
148–132 Gifted/Superior Intelligence
115 Higher Than Usual Intelligence
99 Average Intelligence
83 Low Average Intelligence
70 or below Very Low Intelligence

CHAPTER 8

GEOMETRY

G.F. Bernhard Riemann
(1826-1886)

G.F. Bernhard Riemann was about 14 years old when the director of his school noticed that he had an aptitude for mathematics. He loaned Bernhard some of his books, including a 900-page tome on the theory of numbers, which the boy read in only six days.

When he went to the University at Gottingen, however, Riemann did not make much of an impression on his professors. Riemann was a prodigy who had a kind of instinct about math—he could "see" almost instantaneously solutions to problems that others were forced to work out for themselves on paper. His gift is called "intuitive reasoning," but in a university setting the faculty required their students to support their conclusions with mathematical proofs, and Riemann really couldn't be bothered.

After he graduated, mathematics became Riemann's life's work. He developed a new type of geometry known ever since as Riemannian geometry. It is a highly abstract field that would boggle the mind of high school geometry students, but it made possible Albert Einstein's theory of relativity. He also advanced theories regarding two-dimensional planes known as Riemann surfaces. And there were many more contributions to number theory, trigonometry, and algebraic geometry.

In 1886 Riemann traveled to Italy, hoping the warm climate would cure him of tuberculosis. He died in Italy. Back home in Gottingen, his housekeeper tidied up his office. As she cleaned, she collected dusty piles of papers and tossed them out. No one knows what Riemann discoveries were lost that day.

✏️ Geometry 1

1 Count the triangles in this figure.

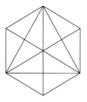

2 This is the design and measurements for a table. How much is necessary to build 30 tables of the same size and shape?

70 cm

30 cm

20 cm   20 cm

3 Is the area for these two parallelograms equal?

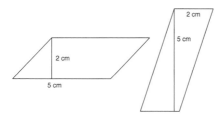

2 cm

5 cm

2 cm

5 cm

4 Each of the three sides of triangle A are twice the length of each of the three sides of triangle B. How many times will triangle B fit inside triangle A?

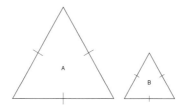

5 l, or length, is 20cm
w, or width, is 30cm
h, or height, is 20cm
If the height of the box is reduced by 30% but the length
remains the same, what will be the new measurements of
the height and the width?

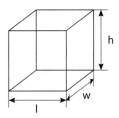

6 The 6 lines divide this triangle into 16 sections. If two more
lines are added, one from each of the two vertices, how
many sections will there be?

7 The radius of the circle is 5. Each side of the pentagon
measures 5.88. What is the area of the pentagon?

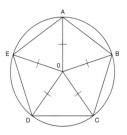

8 Angle A is 120 degrees. Angle B is 90 degrees. Angle D is 2/3 of Angle C. What is the measurement of Angle D and Angle C?

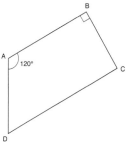

9 Count the faces, edges, and vertices of this figure.

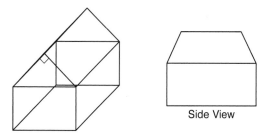

Side View

10 How many cubes are needed to make a stairway 9 cubes high?

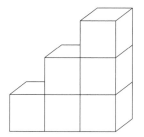

ANSWERS ·····································

① 37 triangles

② 8100cm^2 of wood

③ Yes. By multiplying the base and the height of one and height and base of the other you reach the same answer—10cm.

④ 4 times

⑤ height = 52 cm; width = 23.08 cm

⑥ 25 sections

⑦ 59.54

⑧ Angle D is 60 degrees; Angle C is 90 degrees.

⑨ 17 edges, 9 faces, 10 vertices

⑩ 45 cubes

SCORING ·····································

Award 16.5 points for each correct answer.

165 Genius
148–132 Gifted/Superior Intelligence
115 Higher Than Usual Intelligence
99 Average Intelligence
83 Low Average Intelligence
70 or below Very Low Intelligence

✏️ Geometry 2

1 How many triangles can you draw from the 5 points on the edge of this circle?

2 On this gift, 47 cm of ribbon has been used to make the bow. What is the length of ribbon used on the box, including the bow? Give your answer in meters.

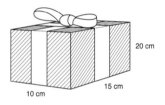

20 cm

15 cm

10 cm

3 Angle PRQ measures 120 degrees. Angle PST measures 110 degrees. What is the measurement in degrees of Angle RPS?

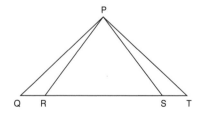

P

Q   R   S   T

4 What is the length of side LM in millimeters?

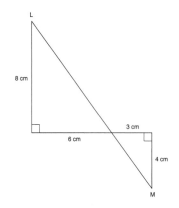

5 In this parallelogram, AB is 20 cm long. AE is 3 cm long. FC is 3 cm long. What is the length of DF?

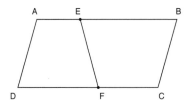

6 Angle is AOB is 132 degrees. Angle COD is 141 degrees. What is the measurement of angle DOB?

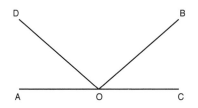

7. Given the information in the drawing, what is the measurement of angle MBD?

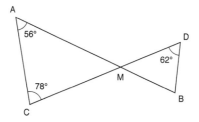

8. All of the squares inside the rectangle are the same size. If the area of the rectangle equals 432 square cm, what is the perimeter?

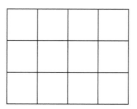

9. The area of this trapezoid is 400 square cm. What is the height of line h?

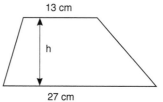

⑩ ABCD is a parallelogram. Given the information in the figure, what are the coordinates of point D?

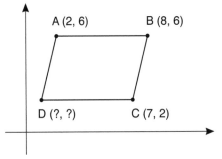

ANSWERS ·

① 10 triangles
② 177 cm = 1.77 m
③ 50 degrees
④ 150 mm
⑤ 17 cm

⑥ 93 degrees
⑦ 72 degrees
⑧ 84 cm
⑨ 20 cm
⑩ (1, 2)

SCORING ·

Award 16.5 points for each correct answer.

165 Genius
148–132 Gifted/Superior Intelligence
115 Higher Than Usual Intelligence
99 Average Intelligence
83 Low Average Intelligence
70 or below Very Low Intelligence

CHAPTER 9

CALCULATING SIMPLE INTEREST AND COMPOUND INTEREST

Alan Turing
(1912-1954)

As a young boy Alan Turing's teachers recognized that he was precocious, particularly in mathematics and the sciences. All of them encouraged him, except the teachers and headmaster of the Sherbourne School, in which he enrolled when he was 14. Sherbourne's curriculum placed heavy emphasis on mastering Latin and studying the literature of ancient Rome. Alan didn't care about the Roman classics at all—he wanted to immerse himself in mathematics. Although he had never learned even elementary calculus, he could solve extremely complex math problems.

In spite of the objections of his teachers, Turing did devote himself to mathematics, eventually earning a doctorate from Princeton University in the United States. It was while he was at Princeton that he developed an interest in cryptology, the study of codes. Back in England, he found a job working at the Government Code and Cypher School.

When World War II broke out in 1939, Turling went to work at Bletchley Park, a country estate that the British government had converted into a top-secret research site. Here, some of the most brilliant mathematicians and cryptographers in the country assembled to break the Nazis' codes, particularly the Enigma code, considered the most devilishly complicated cipher ever devised. Previously, codebreakers had approached ciphers as if translating a foreign language, but Turling and his fellow researchers knew that the Nazi ciphers were infinitely more sophisticated, so they used mathematical analysis to break the code.

Turing not only found the key to unlocking the Enigma code, but also the key to the code used by the Nazi navy, which led to an Allied victory in the battle for the Atlantic.

After the war Turing began creating the forerunner of computers. In 1952 he was arrested and tried for homosexual activity—at the time, such activity was illegal in England. Although for his cryptography work he had been made an Officer in the Order of the British Empire, his conviction in a criminal trial meant that he lost his government security clearance. The court gave him the option of either serving time in prison, or submitting to a hormonal treatment intended to suppress his libido. Turing opted for the hormonal treatment. Two years later Turing's housekeeper found him dead—he had killed himself with a fatal dose of cyanide.

✏️ Simple Interest 1

1. A student borrows $850 at a simple interest rate of 7.5%. He promises to repay the loan in 4 months. How much interest will be owed when the loan is due?

2. A company borrows $1180 at a simple interest rate of 11.3%. Repayment of the loan is due in 60 days. What is the total amount—original loan plus interest—due after 60 days?

3. A woman wrote a check for $5460, which paid off money she had borrowed at a simple interest rate of 7.5% for 8 months. How much was the original loan?

4. A man borrowed $3200. Ninety days later he repaid the loan, with interest, with a check for $3276.80. What was the simple rate of interest?

5. A loan company charges 12 cents per day for every $100 borrowed. A couple borrows $800. How much will they owe after 50 days?

6. A loan company charges 12 cents per day for every $100 borrowed. A couple borrows $800. After 50 days they pay off the loan with a check for $848. What interest rate did the loan company charge?

7. A man borrows $750 for 4 months at a simple interest rate of 9.5%. How much interest will he pay when the loan is due?

8. A loan company offers $1200 for 60 days at a simple interest rate of 12.4%. What is the total amount—original loan plus interest—due after 60 days?

9 A student wrote a check for $6369, which paid off a student loan she had borrowed at a simple interest rate of 8.2% for 9 months. How much was the original loan?

10 A man borrowed $5400 and 60 days later paid it off with a check for $5502.60. What was the rate of interest?

ANSWERS ·

⑩ 11.4%   **⑤** $848

⑥ $5000   **④** 9.6%

⑧ $1224.80   **③** $5200

⑦ $23.75   **②** $1446.68

⑨ 43.2%   **①** $21.25

SCORING ·

Award 16.5 points for each correct answer.

165 Genius
148–132 Gifted/Superior Intelligence
115 Higher Than Usual Intelligence
99 Average Intelligence
83 Low Average Intelligence
70 or below Very Low Intelligence

✏️ Compound Interest 1

1 An investment of $5000 will receive 4.3% interest, compounded quarterly. How much will the investment be worth in 3 years?

2 What will be the interest on $7500 invested at 3.8%, compounded monthly, for 4 years?

3 $3000 is invested at 4.1%, compounded monthly. How many years will it take for the investment to grow to $5000?

4 After 5 years, with an interest rate of 3.5% compounded semi-annually, an investment account has a balance of $10,110.28. What was the amount of the original investment?

5 $10,000 is invested at an interest rate compounded annually. After years the investment has grown to $11,608.86. What is the annual rate of interest?

6 $8000 is invested at 2.9%, compounded quarterly. What will the investment be worth in 2 years?

7 $9200 is invested at 3.4% compounded monthly for 4 years. How much interest did the investment earn?

8 An investor invests $3000 at 4.6% compounded monthly. How long will it take for the investor to double his money?

9 After 6 years and an interest rate of 4.7% compounded semi-annually, an investment account has a balance of $12,157.44. What was the amount of the original investment?

10 $8000 is invested at an interest rate that is compounded annually. After 3 years, the balance in the account is $9314.02. What is the interest rate?

ANSWERS ·

⑩ 5.2%

⑨ $9200

⑧ 15 years

⑦ $1338.25

⑥ $8475.95

⑤ 3.8%

④ $8500

③ 12.5 years

② 1229.11

① $5684.54

SCORING ·

Award 16.5 points for each correct answer.

165 Genius
148–132 Gifted/Superior Intelligence
115 Higher Than Usual Intelligence
99 Average Intelligence
83 Low Average Intelligence
70 or below Very Low Intelligence

✏ Compound Interest 2

① Every month an investor deposits $300 in an investment account. The account pays 3.2%, compounded monthly. How much will the account be worth in 10 years?

② Once a year an investor deposits $1000 into an account that pays 5%, compounded annually. How much interest will the account earn in 4 years?

③ A company wants to purchase a new piece of equipment that costs $50,000. For 3 years, every quarter the company makes a deposit in an investment account that pays 4.2%

interest, compounded quarterly. How much money must the company deposit each quarter to reach its goal?

④ An investor deposits $300 per month into an account that pays 2.8%, compounded monthly. In months, how long will it take for the account to reach a balance of $10,000?

⑤ Once a year an investor deposits $2000 into an investment account. After 4 years, the balance of the account is $8417.33. What was the annual compounding rate of interest?

⑥ Once a month an investor deposits $400 into an account that pays 3.8% compounded monthly. What is the balance of the account in 8 years?

⑦ Once a year an investor deposits $2000 into an account that pays 4% compounded annually. How much interest will the account earn in 3 years?

⑧ A company wants to buy a piece of equipment that costs $100,000. The company gives itself 5 years to make the purchase. Every quarter the company deposits money in an account that pays 4.7% compounded quarterly. To reach the $100,000 goal, how much must the company deposit each quarter?

⑨ Every month an investor deposits $250 into an account. The account pays 3.5% compounded monthly. In how many months will the account have a balance of $10,000?

⑩ Once a year an investor deposits $3000 into an account. At the end of 5 years the account balance is $15,895.60. What was the annual rate of compounding interest?

A N S W E R S ·

⑩ 2.9%

⑨ 38 months

⑧ $4464.67

⑦ $243.20

⑥ $44,793.88

⑤ 3.4%

④ 33 months

③ $3931.49

② $310.13

① $42,360.90

S C O R I N G ·

Award 16.5 points for each correct answer.

165 Genius
148–132 Gifted/Superior Intelligence
115 Higher Than Usual Intelligence
99 Average Intelligence
83 Low Average Intelligence
70 or below Very Low Intelligence

✎ Simple Interest 2

① A loan company charges 8.6% simple interest for a $690 loan. In 4 months, when repayment is due, how much interest will be owed?

② A student borrows $1900 at 10.8% for 60 days. What is the total amount—loan plus interest—due at that time?

③ A couple paid off a loan with a check for $6812. The loan had an interest rate of 9.6% for 6 months. How much money did the couple borrow?

④ After 120 days, a woman paid off a loan for $2800 with a check in the amount of $2917.60. What was the annual rate of interest?

5 A loan company demands 13 cents per day for every $100 borrowed. A man borrows $500 for 50 days. What amount must he repay?

6 A loan company demands 13 cents per day for every $100 borrowed. A man borrows $500 for 50 days. What rate of interest is the company charging?

7 A teenager opened a bank account with a deposit of $500. The account pays 5% simple interest annually. She never added any money to the account. At the end of 4 years, how much money was in the account?

8 An investor put $1000 in an account that pays 6% interest. After 6 months he withdrew the funds. How much interest did he earn?

9 A child opened a bank account with $147. The account pays simple interest of 1% annually. The child never added any money to the account. What was the balance after 6 years?

10 A bank account has a balance of $839. The bank pays simple interest at an annual rate of 2%. Assuming that no additional funds are deposited into the account, after 15 years, how much interest has accrued?

A N S W E R S ·

10 $252

6 $156

8 $30

7 $600

9 46.8%

5 $532.50

4 12.6%

3 $6500

2 $1934.20

1 $19.78

SCORING ·

Award 16.5 points for each correct answer.

165 Genius
148–132 Gifted/Superior Intelligence
115 Higher Than Usual Intelligence
99 Average Intelligence
83 Low Average Intelligence
70 or below Very Low Intelligence

✏ Compound Interest 3

1 A woman wants to buy a new car. She can afford monthly payments of $350. She wants a 4-year loan at an interest rate of 5.3% compounded monthly. How much will she borrow?

2 A family purchases a $420,000 house. They put down 15% of the purchase price. For the next 30 years they will make equal monthly payments. The rate of interest on their loan is 5.1% compounded monthly. What will be the monthly mortgage payment?

3 A lottery winner deposits $500,000 into an account that pays 4.8% compounded monthly. He will receive monthly payments of $5000. For how many months will he receive these payments?

4 A woman inherits an investment account with a balance of $300,000. Every quarter she withdraws $9443. After 10 years, there is no more money in the account. What was the account's annual compounding rate of interest?

5 A homeowner has a mortgage of $250,000 at 6% compounded monthly. His monthly mortgage payment is

$1754.14. After 20 years, he has paid off the mortgage. How much interest did he pay over those 20 years?

6 A credit card has a balance of $1000. The interest rate is 1.6% per month. The cardholder makes a payment of $80. What is the unpaid balance after that $80 payment?

7 A woman wins $1 million in a lottery. She deposits it all in an account that earns 5.1% compounded annually. She arranges to receive annual payments of $80,000. In how many years will the money run out?

8 A retiree has an account with a balance of $400,000. Every quarter he withdraws $9453. After 15 years the account is empty. What was the account's annual compounding rate of interest?

9 A homeowner has a $220,000 mortgage, at an interest rate of 5.9% compounded monthly. He makes monthly payments of $1404.05. After 25 years the mortgage is paid off. How much interest did he pay over the life of the mortgage?

10 A credit card has a balance of $2000. The interest rate is 1.5% compounded monthly. The cardholder makes a payment of $100. What is the unpaid balance on the card?

ANSWERS ·

⑩ $1930

⑨ $201,215

⑧ 4.9%

⑦ 20 years

⑥ $936

⑤ $170,993.60

④ 4.7%

③ 128 months

② $1938.33

① $15,108.72

SCORING ·

Award 16.5 points for each correct answer.

165 Genius
148–132 Gifted/Superior Intelligence
115 Higher Than Usual Intelligence
99 Average Intelligence
83 Low Average Intelligence
70 or below Very Low Intelligence

CHAPTER 10

MEAN AND MEDIAN
OF NUMBER SETS

Andrew Wiles
(1953-)

Andrew Wiles grew up in universities: when he was born his father was chaplain at Cambridge University's Ridley Hall; Dr. Wiles would move his family to Oxford University, where he was named Regius Professor of Divinity.

From an early age it was clear that Andrew would not follow his father into the ministry. "I was a ten year old and one day I happened to be looking in my local public library and I found a book on maths," he recalled. "It told a bit about the history of [Fermat's Last Theorem] and I, a ten year old, could understand it. From that moment I tried to solve it myself, it was such a challenge, such a beautiful problem." Young Andrew had stumbled upon one of the most famous mathematical puzzles in history, a theorem that the greatest minds had wrestled with—always unsuccessfully—since 1647.

Wiles studied mathematics at Oxford, then went to Cambridge for his doctorate. Although he had never lost his interest in the still-unsolved Fermat's Last Theorem, he decided not to write his dissertation on the problem because he had not yet solved it, and he had no idea how long it might take to find the solution.

In fact, Wiles did not find the proof for Fermat until 1994—fourteen years after receiving his doctorate. The solution made Wiles an international celebrity, with scientific organizations across the globe vying with each other to present him with the most distinguished awards. Even after he received a knighthood from Queen Elizabeth II, Wiles stayed grounded. "I had this very rare privilege of being able to pursue in my adult life what had been my childhood dream," he said. "It's more rewarding than anything one can imagine."

✏️ The Mean of a Set of Numbers 1

1. Five fishermen are standing on a wharf. Their ages are 35, 42, 38, 49, and 36. What is the mean age of the fishermen?

2. Frances' scores on her English tests are 86, 87, 78, 84, 90, and 76. What is her mean score?

3. Alex went shopping four days this week. Monday he spent $15. Tuesday he spent $7. Wednesday he spent $27. Thursday he spent $71. What is the mean of Alex's spending spree?

4. In the last six baseball seasons, Nathaniel hit 14, 21, 18, 23, 15, and 29 doubles. What is the mean of doubles Nathanial hit each season?

5. Roger bowls for his company's team. In his first three matches he scored 95, 110, and 101. There is only one match left, and he wants to have a season mean of 105. What must he bowl in the final game?

6. The heights of a group of six neighborhood kids are: 5'2", 4'7", 5'2", 4'9", 5'1", 4'11". What is the mean height of the children?

7. Five New York City cabbies returned to the garage simultaneously. Their mileages that day were 211.5, 179.3, 192.8, 202.7, and 158.6. What was the mean mileage of the cabbies?

8. Dominic has six tomato plants. He's counted the fruit on each plant: 27, 19, 38, 41, 32, 46. What is the mean number of tomatoes on the plants?

9 In a matter of days five dogs at a kennel had puppies. The litters numbered 6, 5, 7, 3, and 8 puppies. What was in the mean number of puppies per litter?

10 A waitress worked four shifts at a restaurant. Her tips were $215, $187, $255, and $203. What was the mean of her tips?

ANSWERS ·

10 $215

9 5.8 puppies

8 33.83 tomatoes

7 188.98

6 5 feet

5 114 points

4 20 doubles

3 $30

2 83.5

1 40

SCORING ·

Award 16.5 points for each correct answer.

165 Genius
148–132 Gifted/Superior Intelligence
115 Higher Than Usual Intelligence
99 Average Intelligence
83 Low Average Intelligence
70 or below Very Low Intelligence

The Median of a Set of Numbers 1

1 The ages of the Walsh cousins are 19, 25, 24, 30, and 26. What is the median age?

② Books on an art course syllabus cost $29.95, $99.95, $49.75, $98.49, and $19.95. What is the median price of the books?

③ The tallest girls in the dance class stand 5'8", 5'7", 5'9", 5'6', and 5'11". What is the median height of the girls?

④ Seven members of a softball team are on the bench. Their weights are: 198, 231, 174, 189, 201, 211, 193. What is the median weight?

⑤ Seven used cars are lined up side by side on a lot. Their lengths are: 10'2", 8'9", 12', 7'5", 9'11", 8'5", 11'4". What is the cars' median length?

⑥ Five campers collected wood for a campfire. Each returned with a different number of logs: 5, 11, 3, 13, 9. What is the median number of logs collected by the campers?

⑦ Brian has taken the LSAT exam five times his scores are: 333, 702, 450, 669, 398. What's his median score?

⑧ Seven change purses are in a lost and found, each with a different sum of cash inside: $1.25, $5.43, $10, $6.35, $.71, $4.65, $5.50. What is the median amount in the change purses?

⑨ Five college roommates got up at different times: 5:30, 8:15, 10:00, 6:10, 7:15. What was the median time the roommates got up?

⑩ Seven appetizers are offered to restaurant patrons during Happy Hour. The prices are $2.95, $5.49, $6.19, $2.50, $2.49, $.95, and $4.45. What is the median price of the appetizers?

ANSWERS ·

⑩ $2.95

⑨ 7:15

⑧ $5.43

⑦ 450

⑥ 9

⑤ 9.11"

④ 198

③ 5.8"

② $49.75

① 25

SCORING ·

Award 16.5 points for each correct answer.

165 Genius
148–132 Gifted/Superior Intelligence
115 Higher Than Usual Intelligence
99 Average Intelligence
83 Low Average Intelligence
70 or below Very Low Intelligence

✏ The Mean of a Set of Numbers 2

① Eric has memorized the significant events associated with seven dates: 1066, 1215, 1492, 1607, 1776, 1939, 2001. What is the mean of these dates?

② Catherine is shopping for car insurance. She has collected five quotes: $550, $675, $299, $325, $510. What is the mean of the insurance quotes?

③ In six districts, voter turn out was unusually high: 799, 623, 581, 809, 851, 767. What was the mean turn out among the districts?

4 Four neighboring vineyards had a difficult summer with low yields. After harvesting and bottling their wine, they had a reduced number of cases of wine for sale: 1023, 966, 802, 1134. What is the mean number of cases available?

5 The six Sundstrom brothers all own farms of various sizes: 600 acres, 1100 acres, 520 acres, 775 acres, 910 acres, 915 acres. What is the mean size of the Sundstroms' farms?

6 Seven high school students had varying degrees of success selling tickets for a school concert: 12, 25, 51, 42, 35, 60, 54. What is the mean of tickets sold?

7 Matt's chemistry test scores for the year are: 91, 89, 85, 94, 92. What is his mean score?

8 Margaret has five rosebushes. During the peak blooming season she counted the blossoms on each bush: 42, 39, 38, 51, 56. What is the mean number of roses in Margaret's garden?

9 A middle school has four classes for fifth graders, each with a different number of students: 19, 25, 21, 22. What is the mean number of students?

10 Five parking garages are almost filled to capacity with cars: 521, 498, 549, 602, 579. What is the mean number of cars parked in the garages?

A N S W E R S ·

⑩ 549.8 cars

⑥ 21.75

⑧ 45.2 roses

⑦ 90.2

⑨ 39.85

⑤ 803.33 acres

④ 981.25

③ 738.33

② $471.80

① 1585.14

SCORING ·

Award 16.5 points for each correct answer.

165 Genius
148–132 Gifted/Superior Intelligence
115 Higher Than Usual Intelligence
99 Average Intelligence
83 Low Average Intelligence
70 or below Very Low Intelligence

✏️ The Median of a Set of Numbers 2

1 In baskets, five farmers collected eggs from a hen house. The number of eggs in the baskets: 14, 12, 19, 7, 21. What is the median number of eggs collected?

2 A rack in a health club holds seven dumb bells weighing 55, 25, 40, 35, 45, 50, and 65 pounds. What is the median weight of the dumb bells?

3 A lighting store offers light bulbs in a variety of wattages: 75, 100, 25, 65, 200, 15, 500. What is the median wattage of the bulbs?

4 A tray holds a handful of coins: 10, 5, 1, 25, 50. What is the median value of the coins?

5 The winning numbers for a lottery were: 11, 39, 62, 7, 35, 58, 94. What is the median number?

6 A graffiti artists has spray painted random numbers on a concrete wall: 77, 33, 90, 101, 69, 14, 82, 638, 13. What is the median number?

7 The ages of a group of children on a playground are 11, 7, 8, 2, 4, 5, 9, 6, and 10. What is the median age of the children?

8 A five-shelf bookcase holds a different number of books on each shelf: 43, 30, 51, 22, 41. What is the median number of books?

9 The colleges of Connecticut's state university system were founded in different years: 1848, 1901, 1973, 1870, 1946, 1898, 1955. What is the median year the colleges were founded?

10 Jars filled with pennies were delivered to a local charity. Each jar held a different number of pennies: 512, 490, 339, 345, 618, 701, 825, 749, 387. What is the median number of pennies in the jars?

ANSWERS ·

10 512 pennies
9 1901
8 41 books
7 7
6 77

5 39
4 10 cents
3 75 watts
2 45 pounds
1 14 eggs

SCORING ·

Award 16.5 points for each correct answer.

165 Genius
148–132 Gifted/Superior Intelligence
115 Higher Than Usual Intelligence
99 Average Intelligence
83 Low Average Intelligence
70 or below Very Low Intelligence